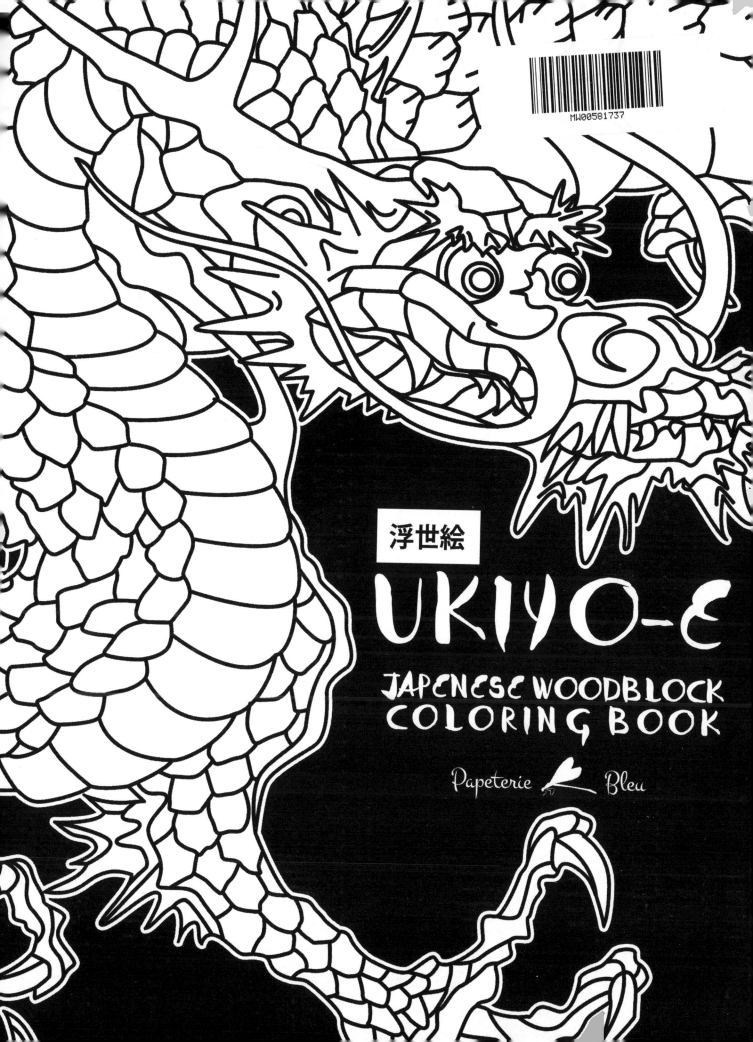

浮世絵

UKIYO-E
JAPENESE WOODBLOCK COLORING BOOK

Papeterie Bleu

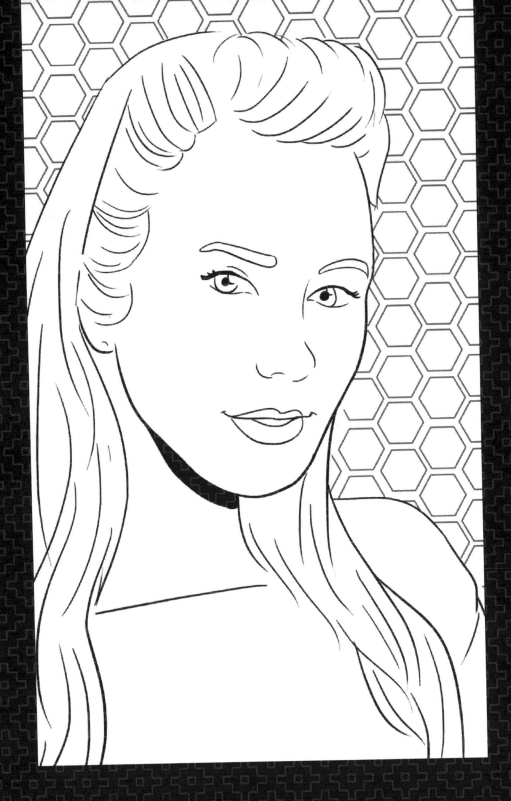

Illustrated by Ekaterina

ISBN-13: 978-1-945888-51-9
ISBN-10: 1-945888-51-2

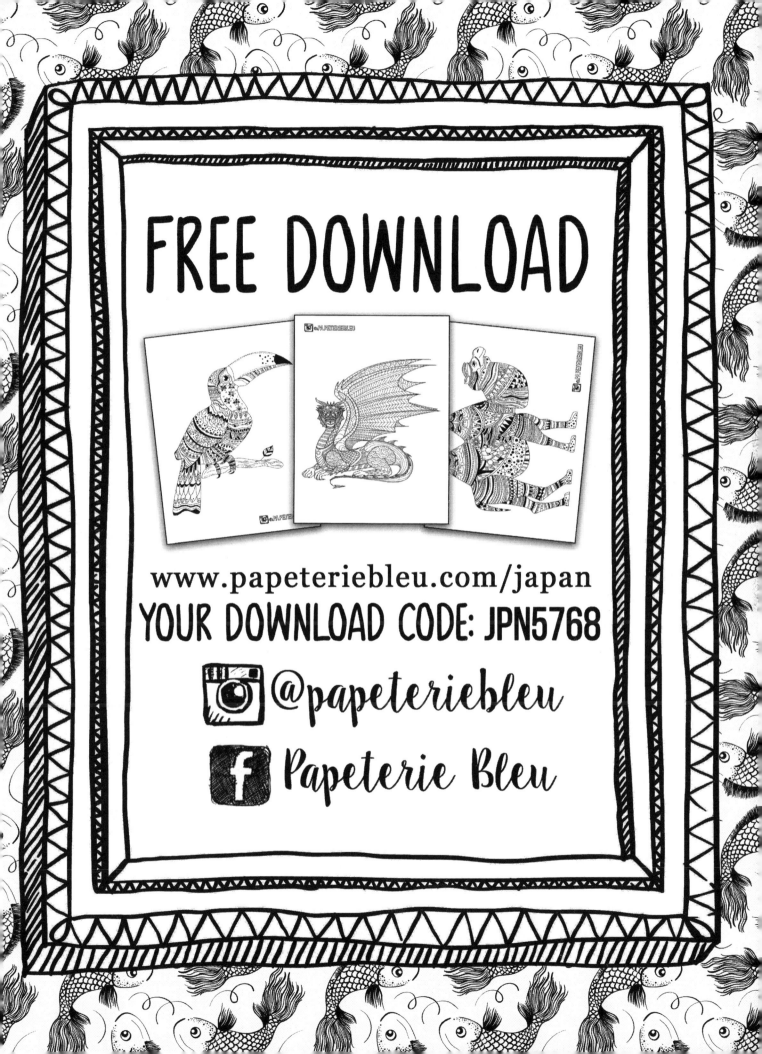

FREE DOWNLOAD

www.papeteriebleu.com/japan

YOUR DOWNLOAD CODE: JPN5768

@papeteriebleu

Papeterie Bleu

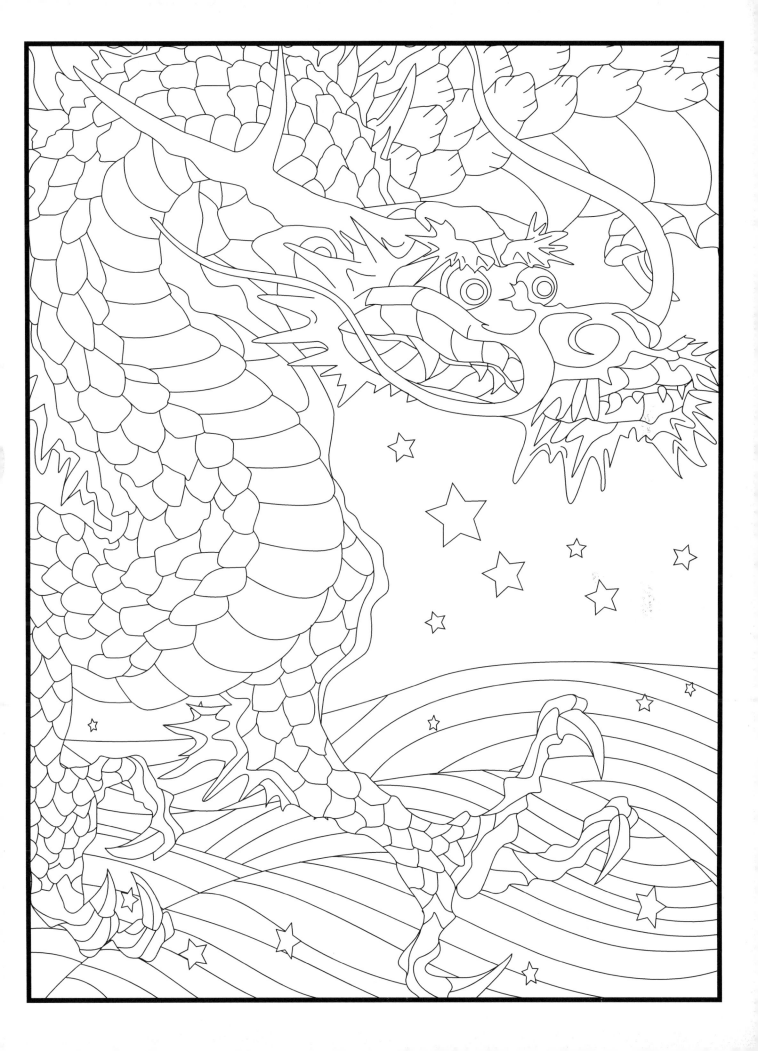

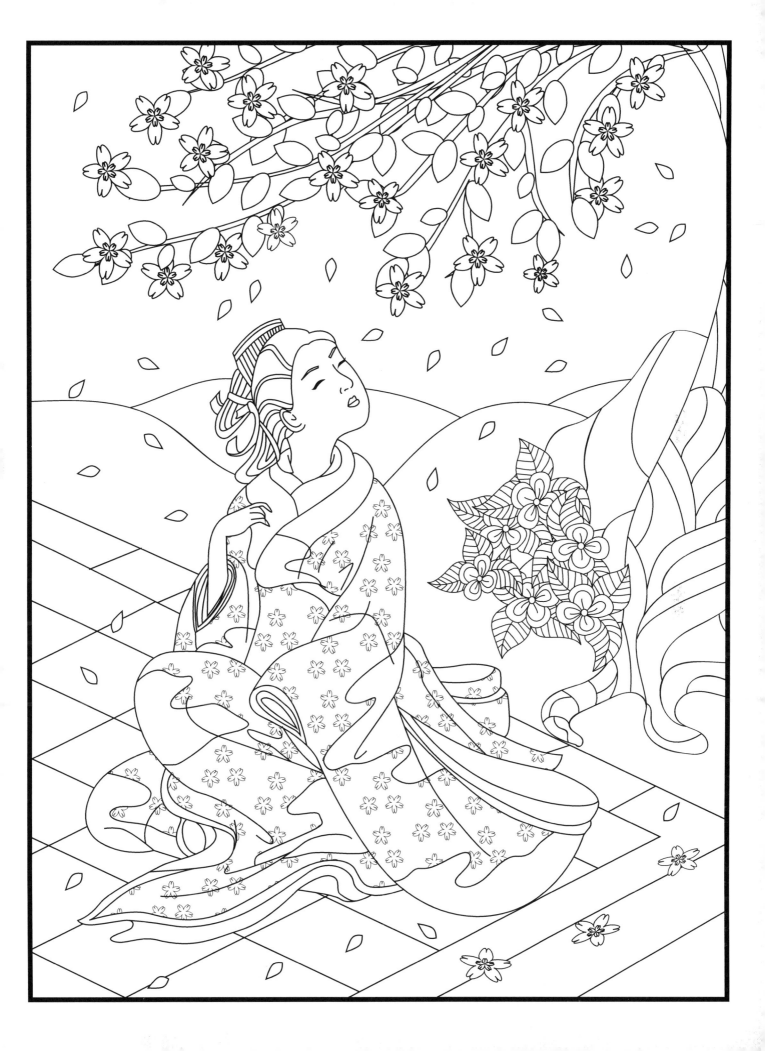

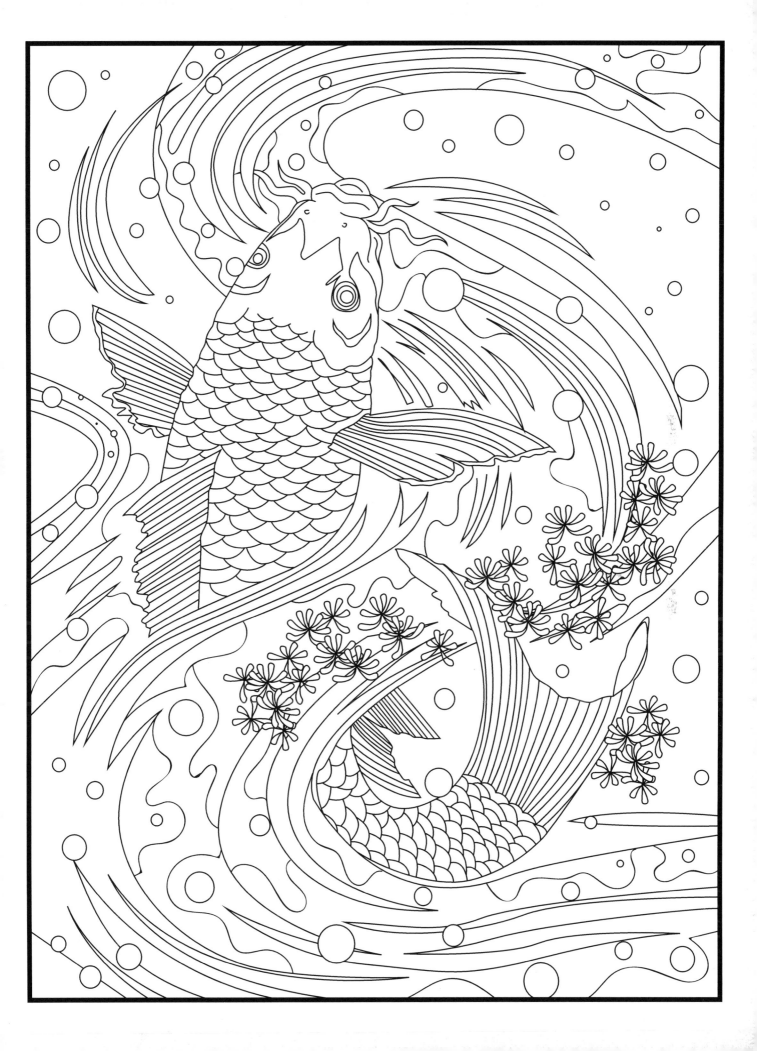

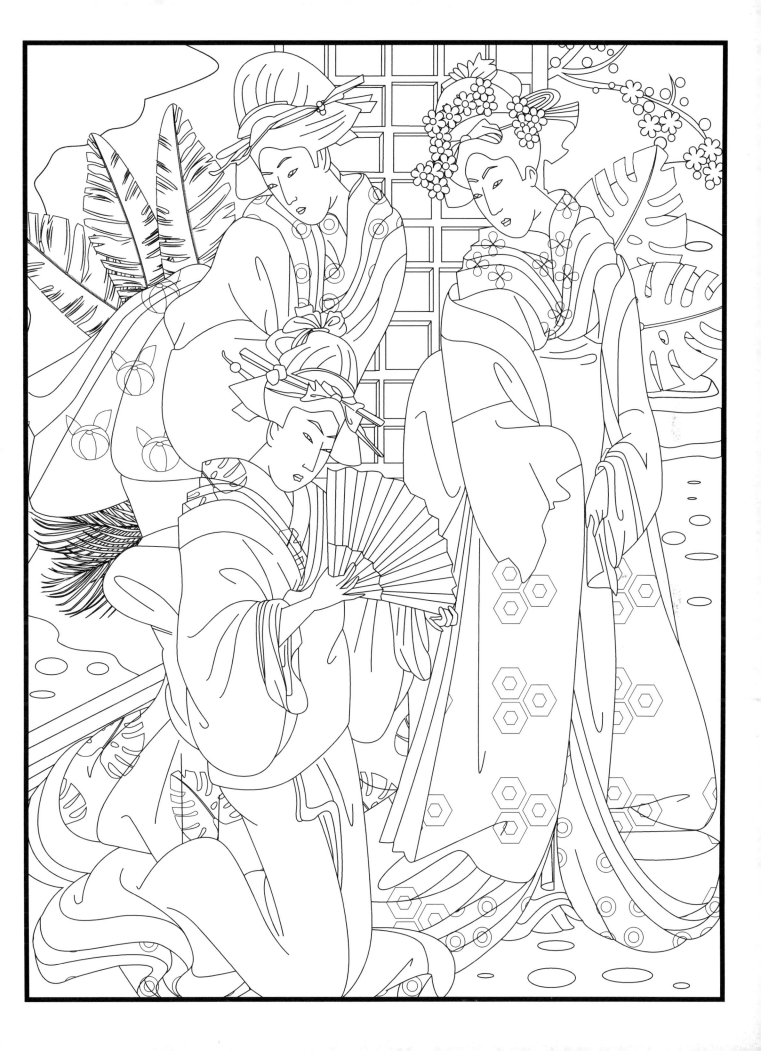

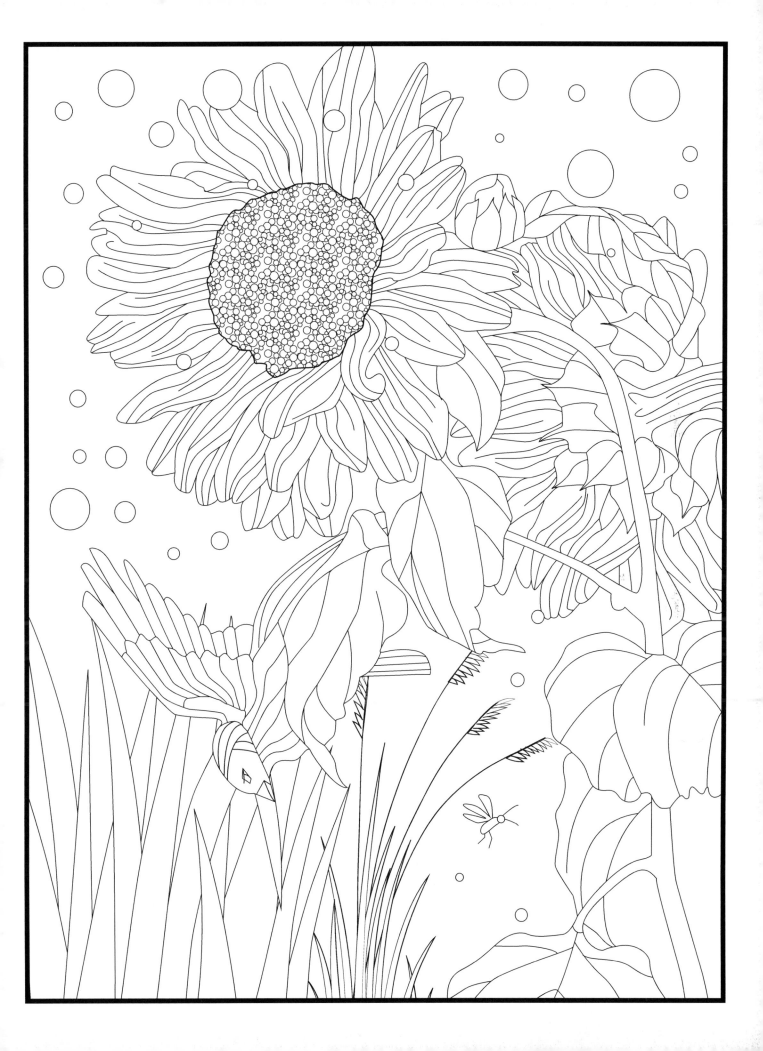

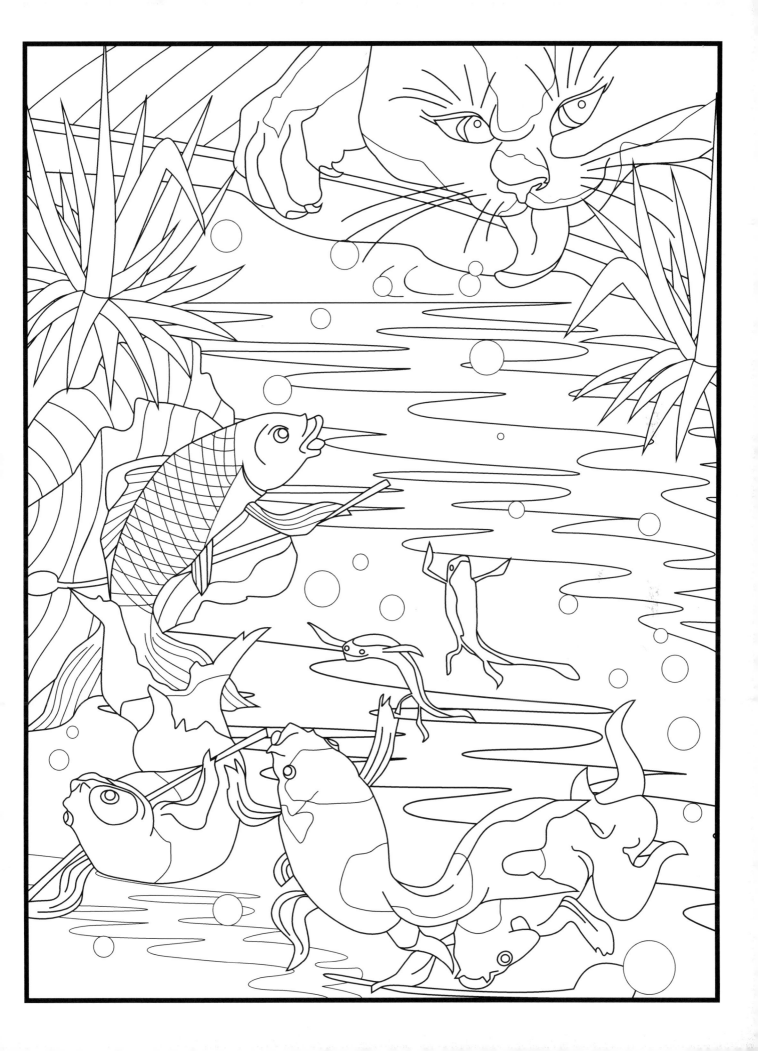

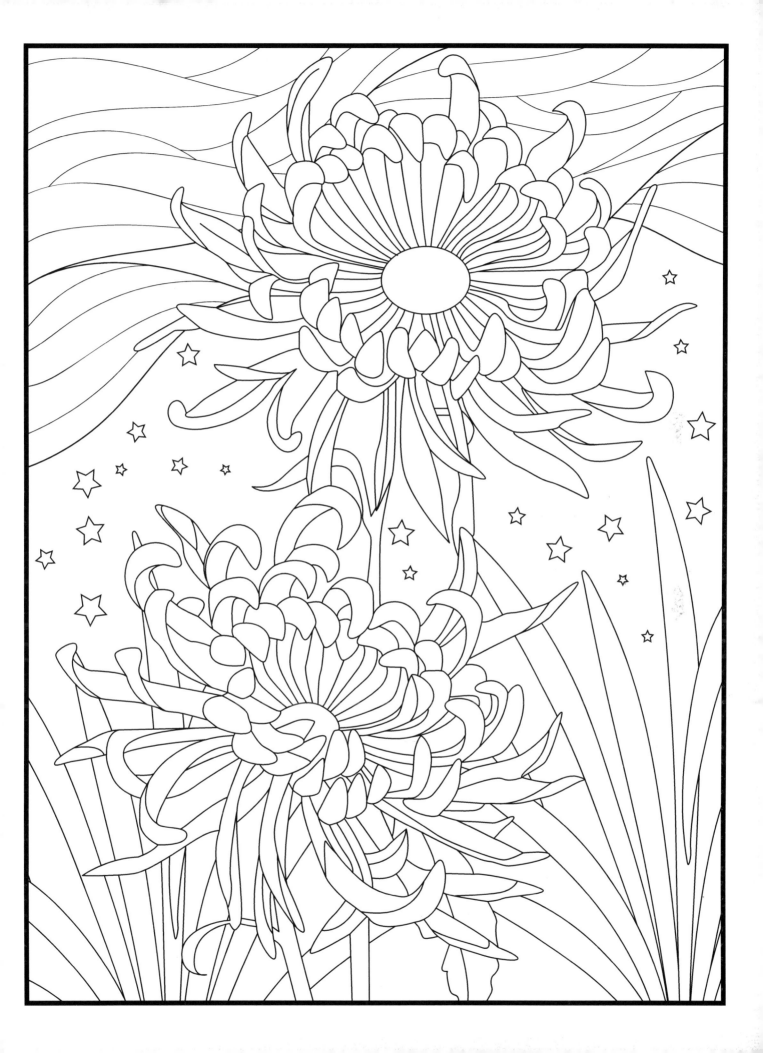

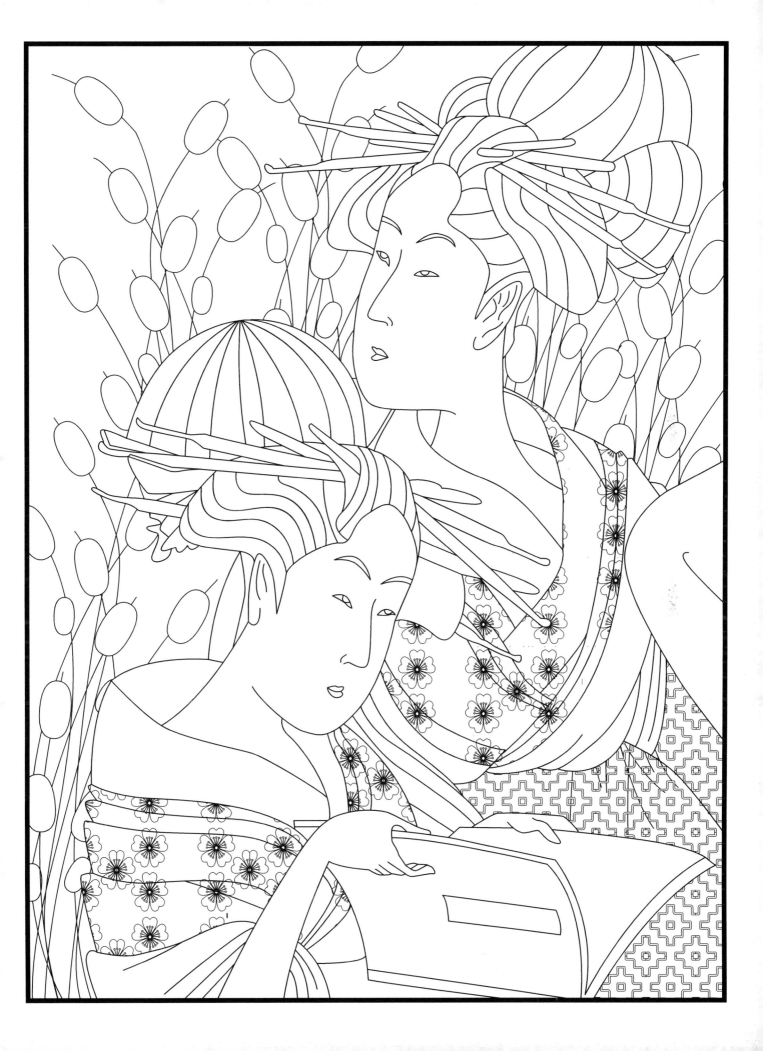

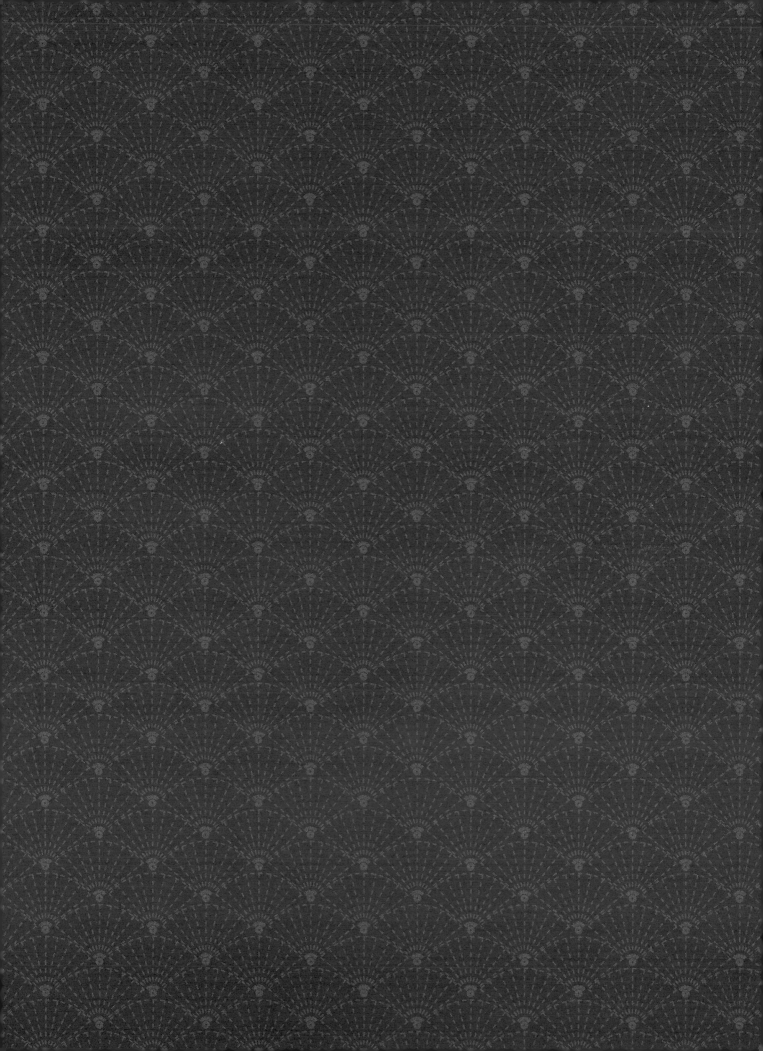

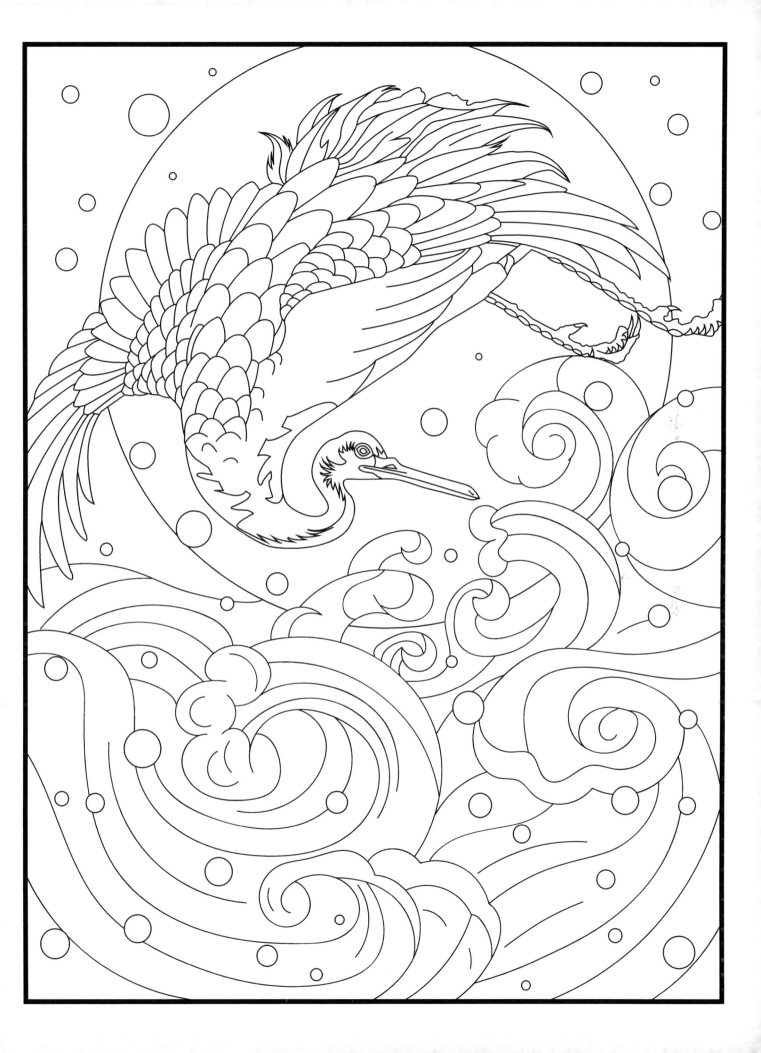

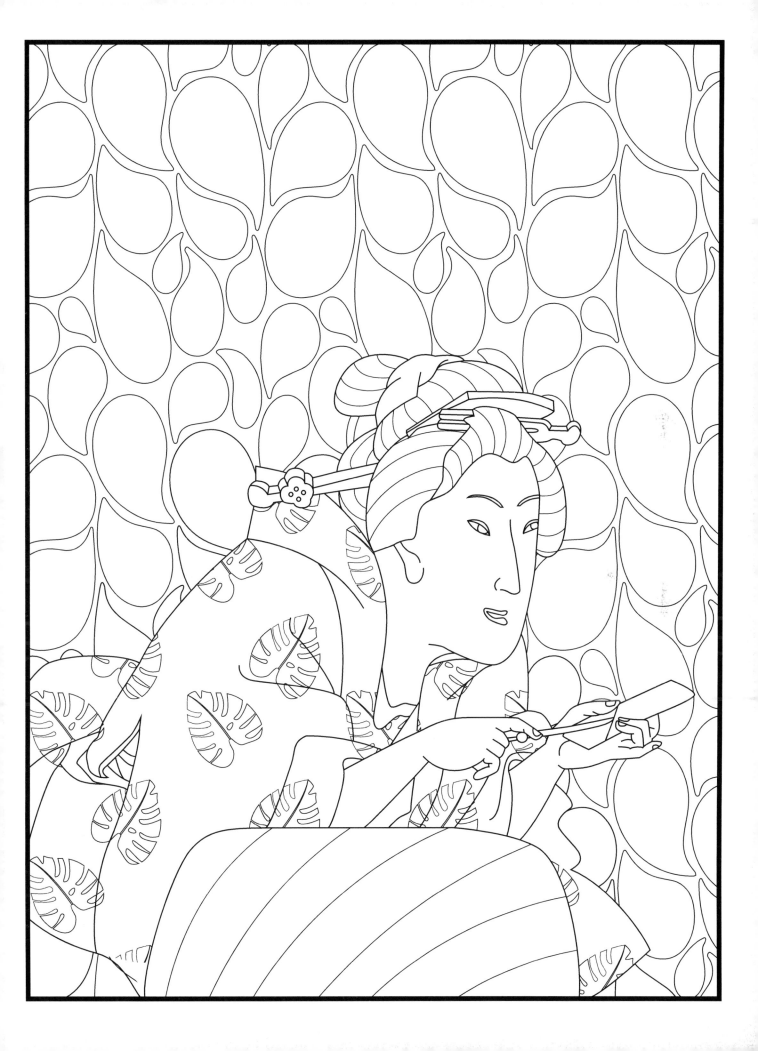

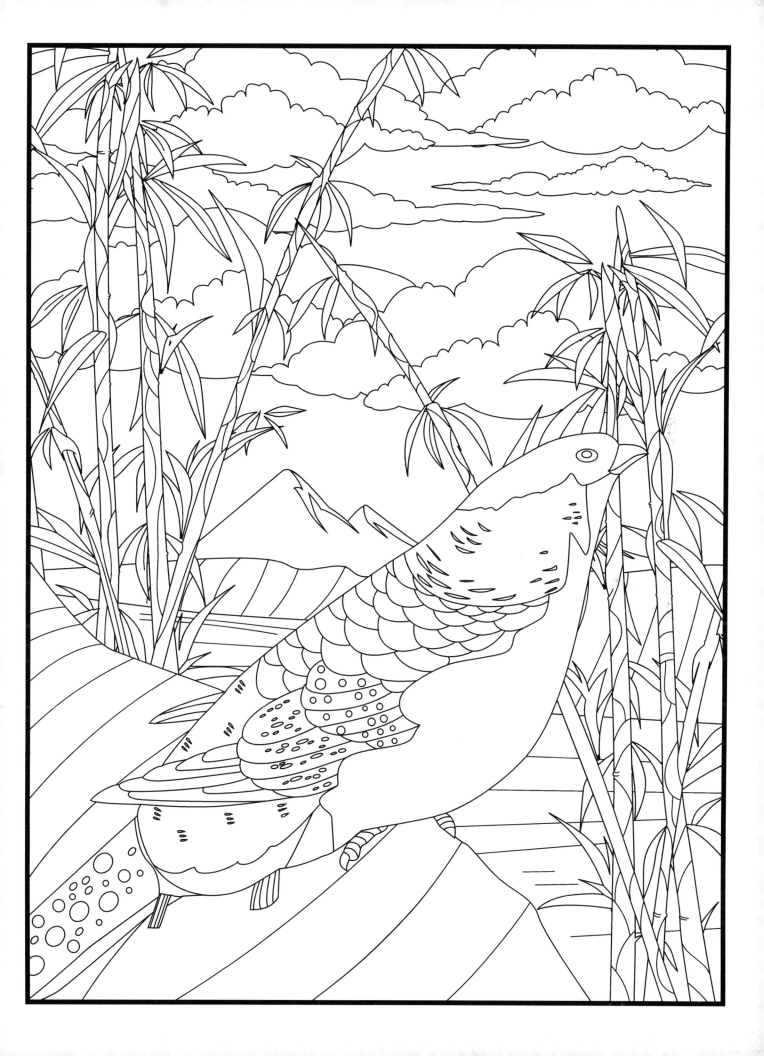

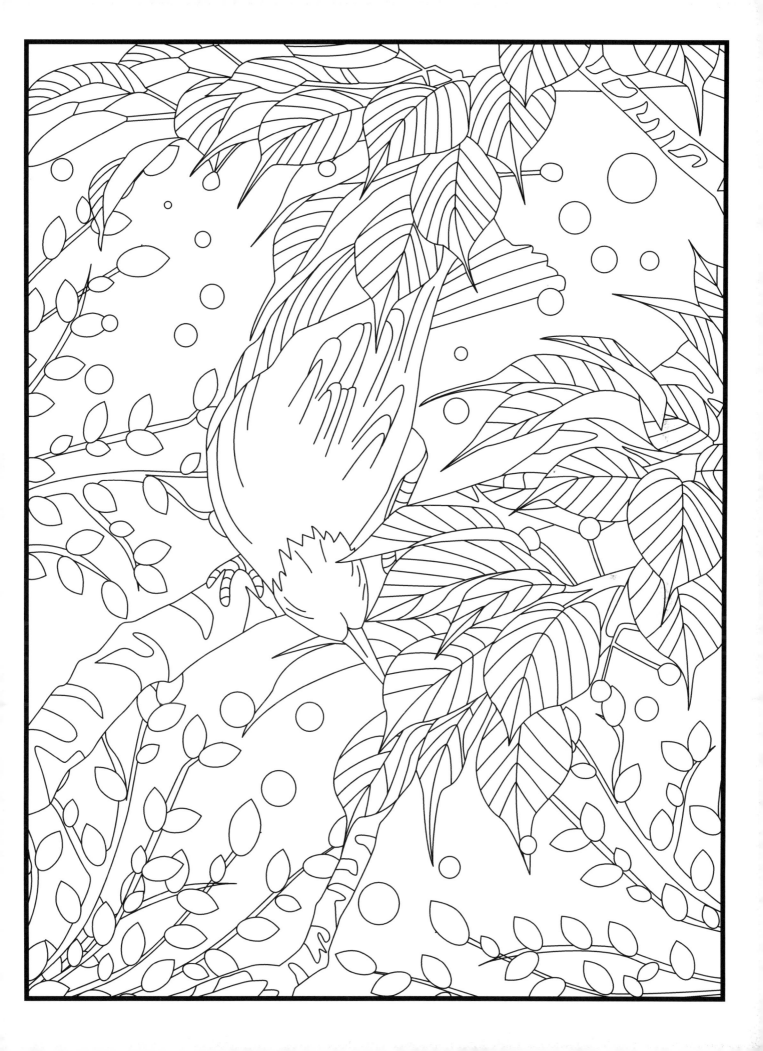

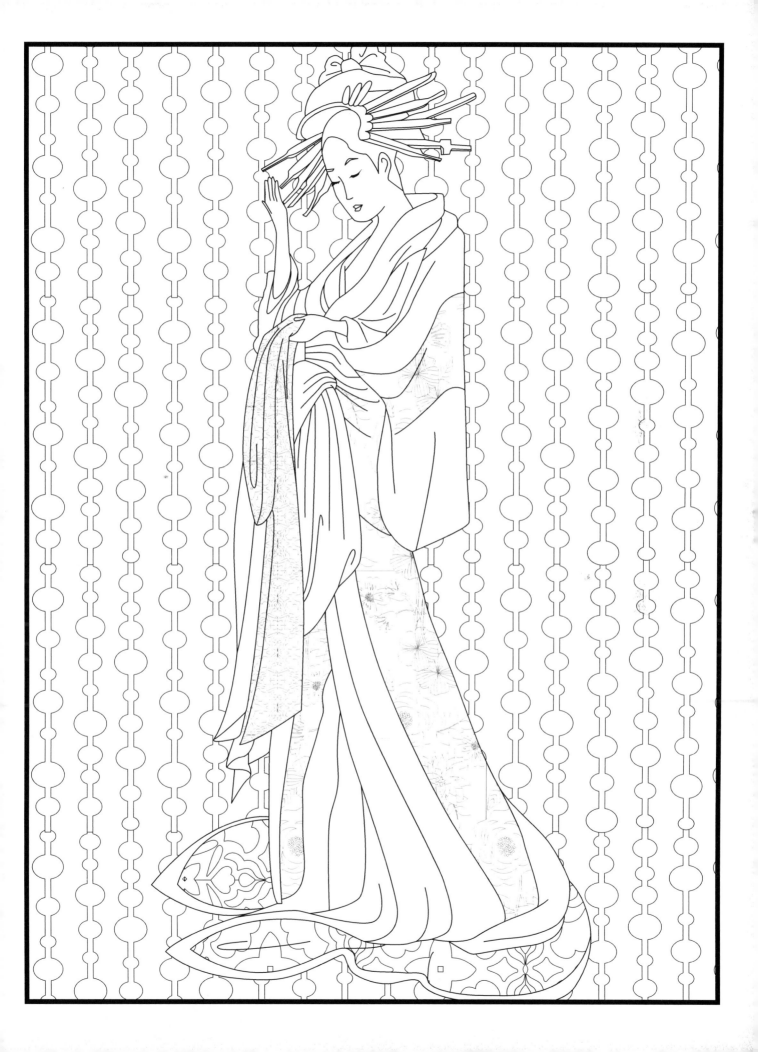

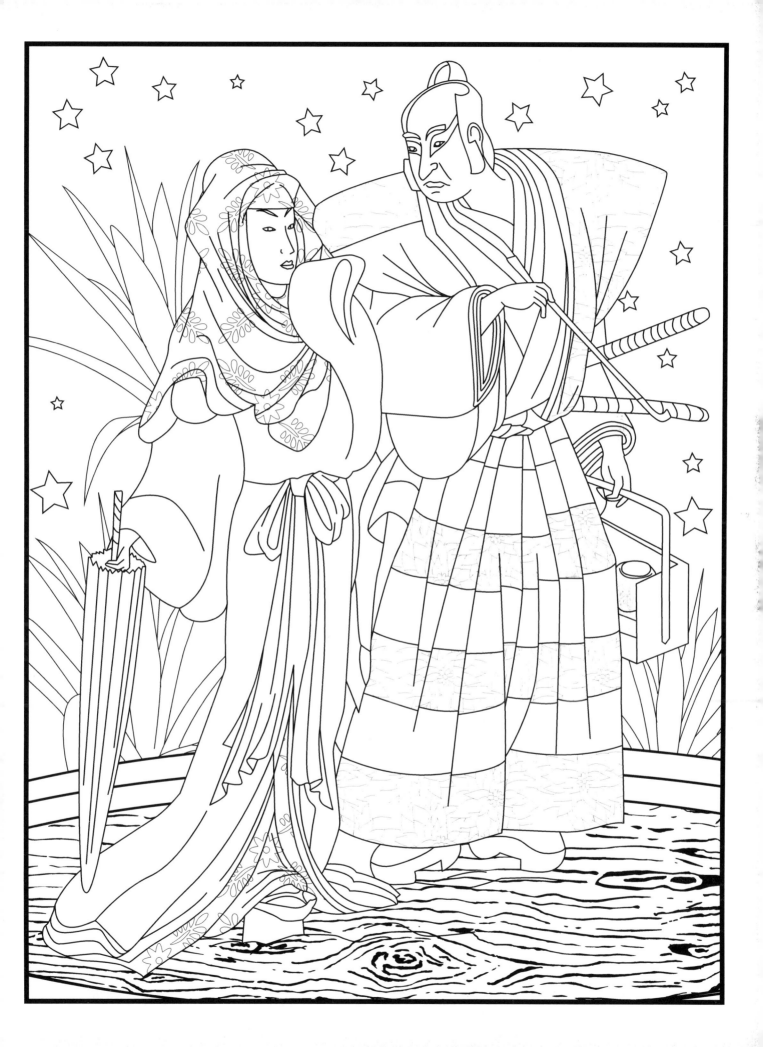

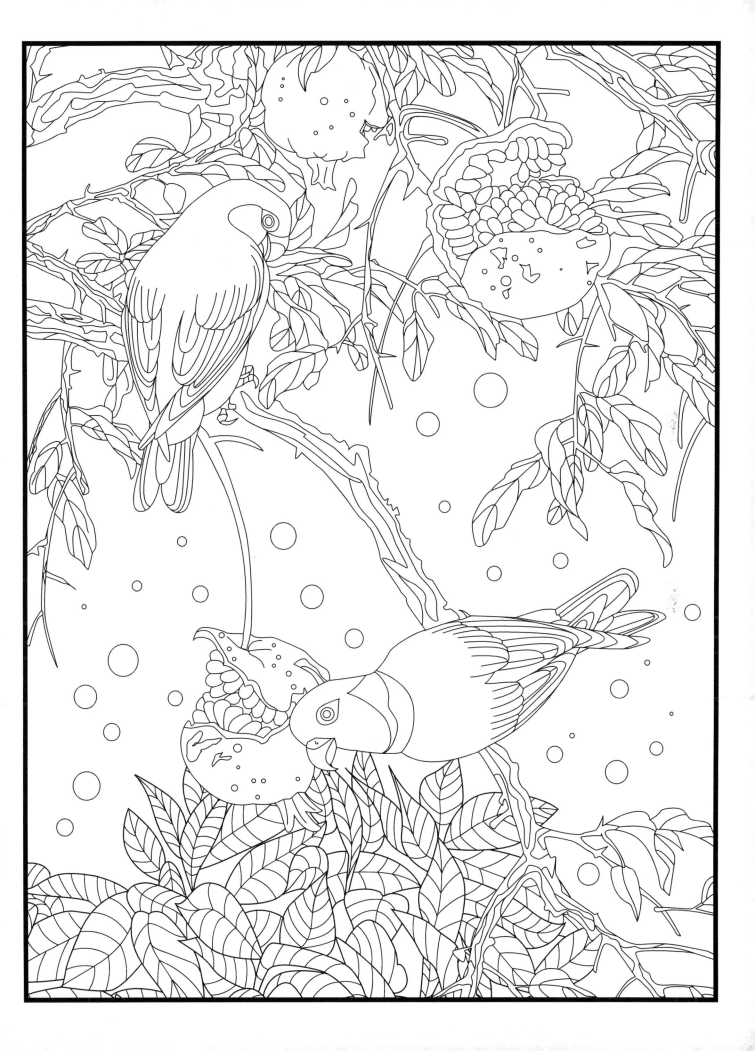

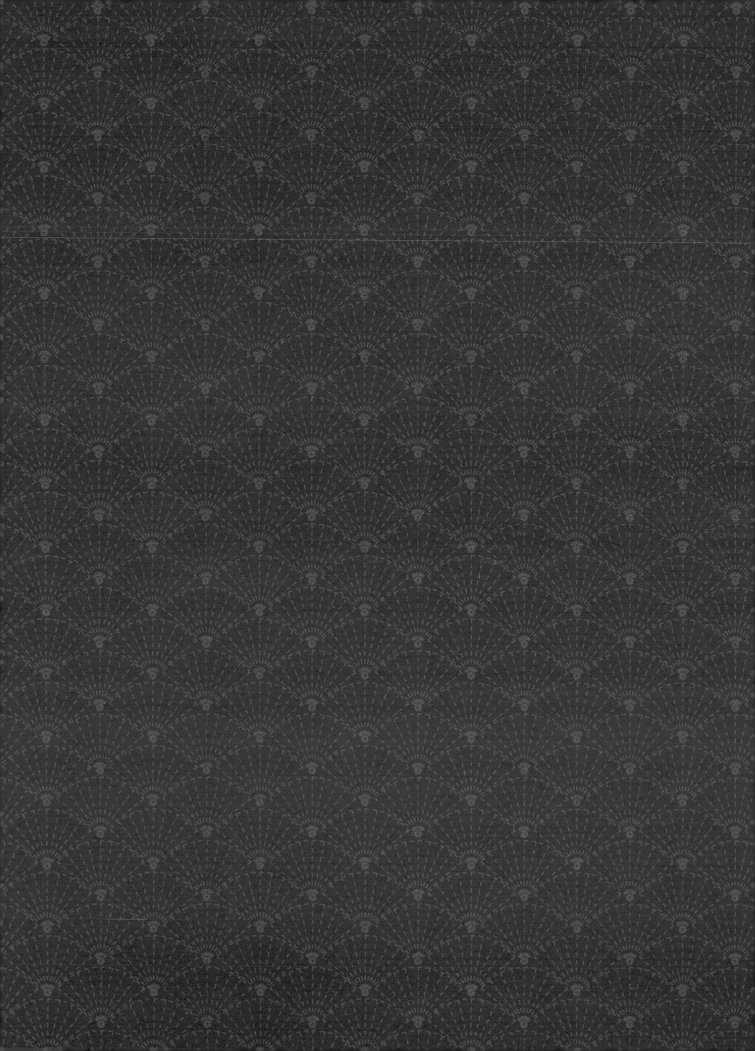

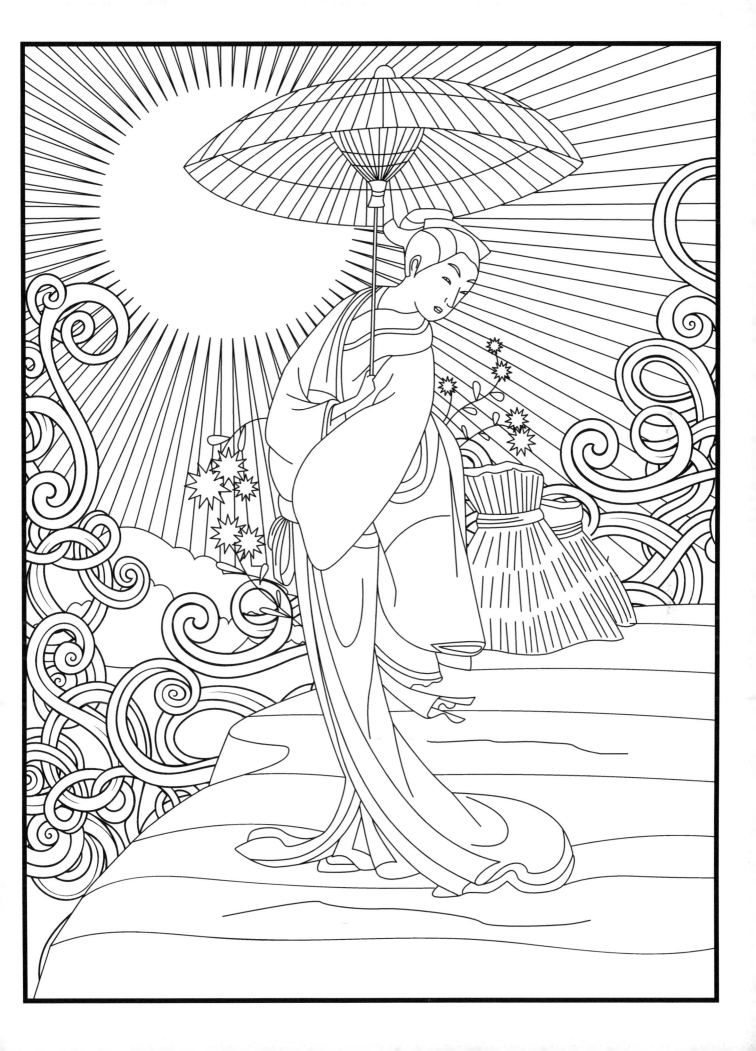

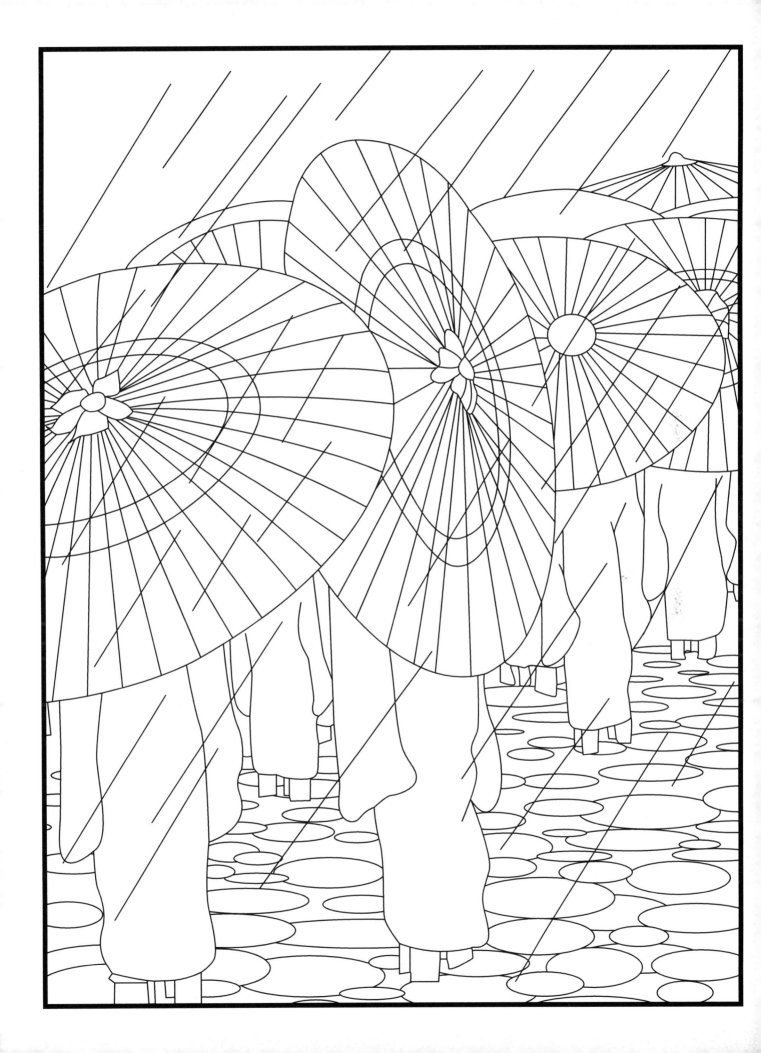

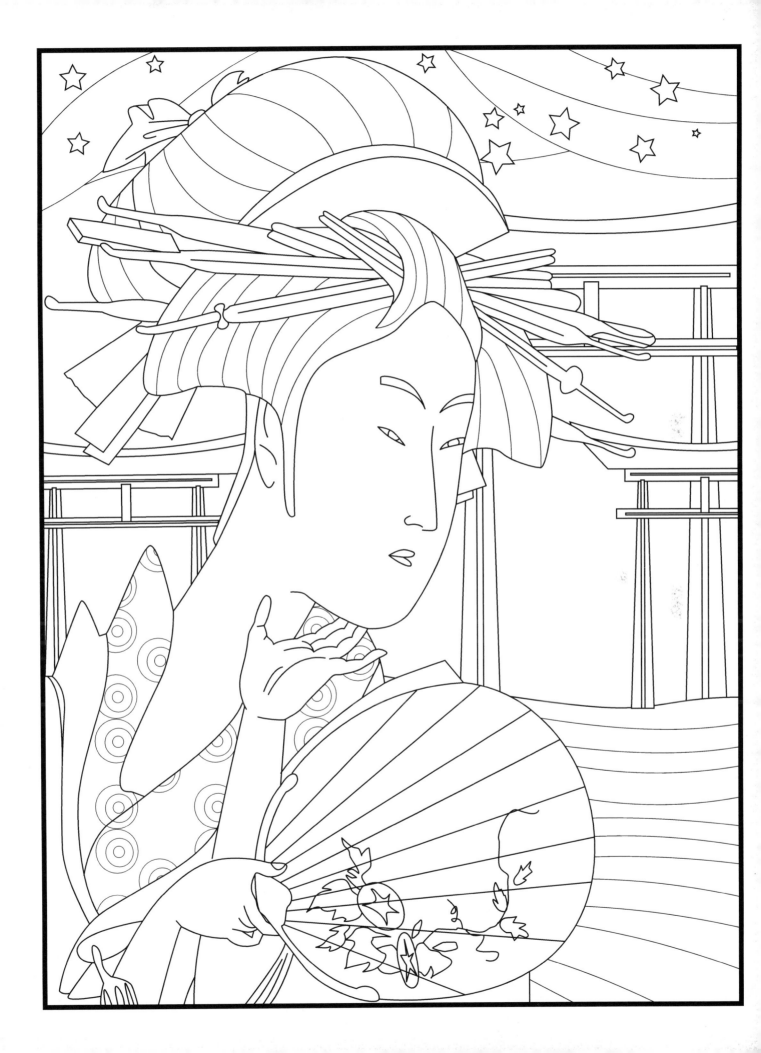

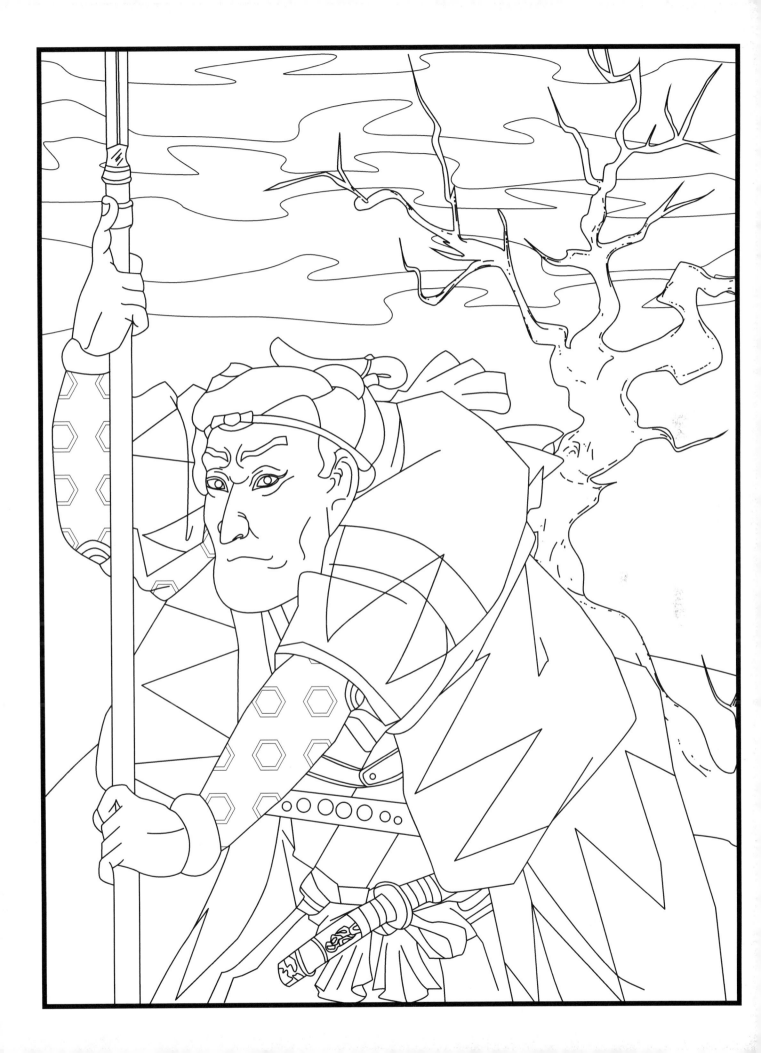

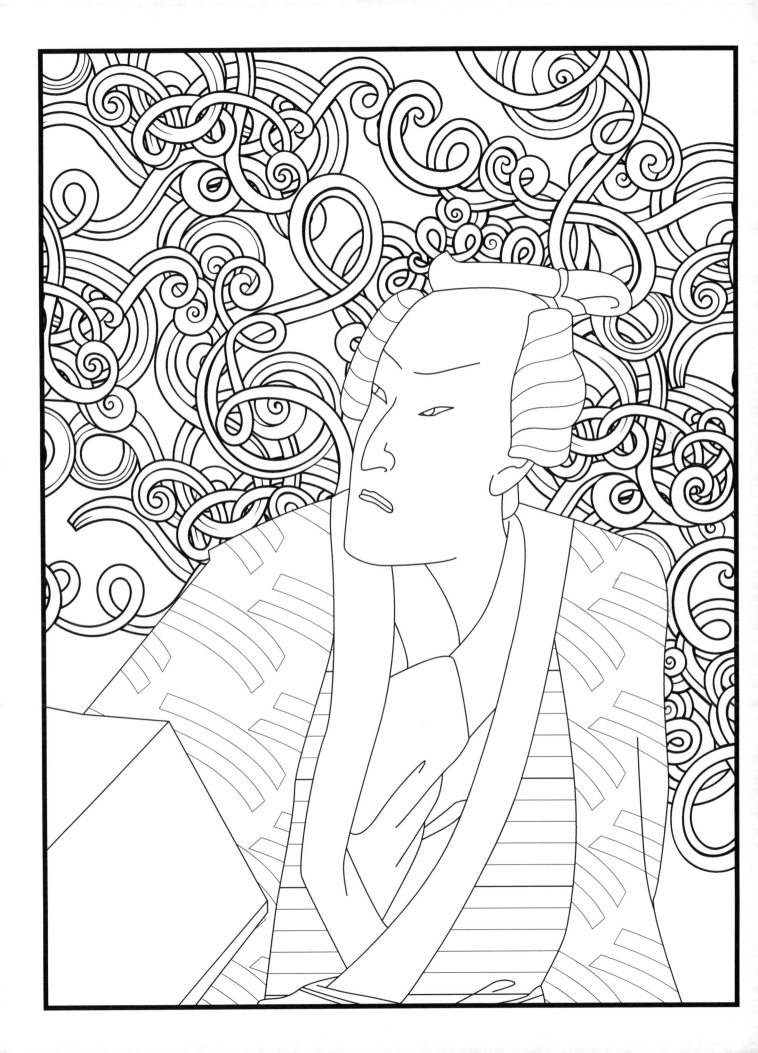

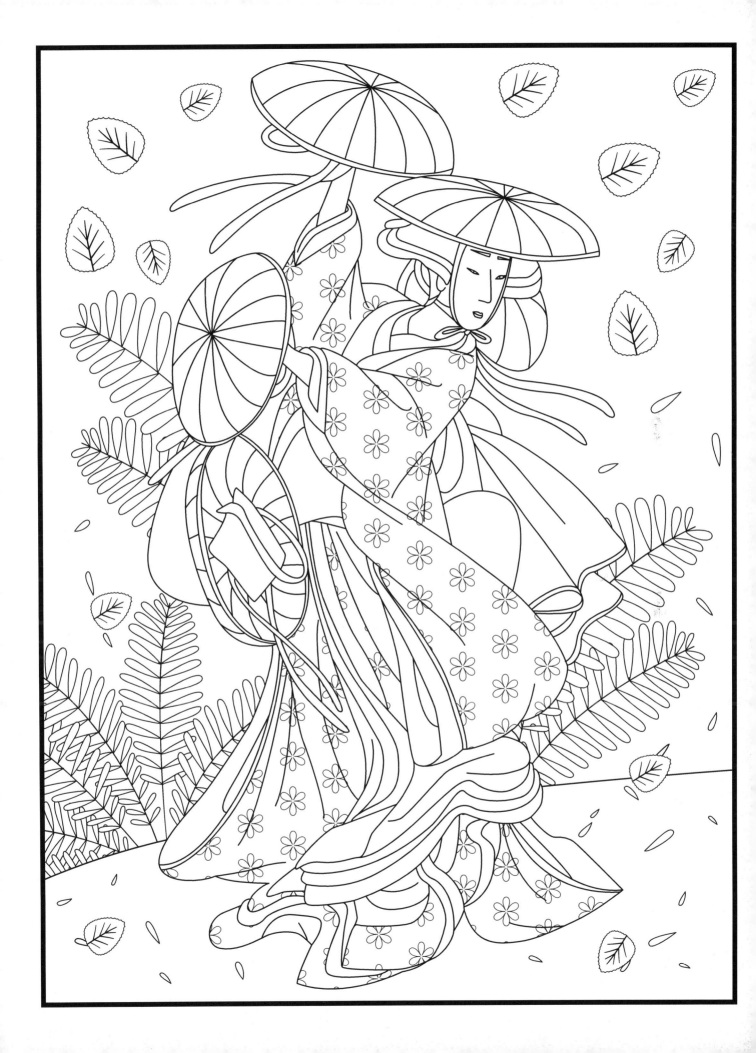

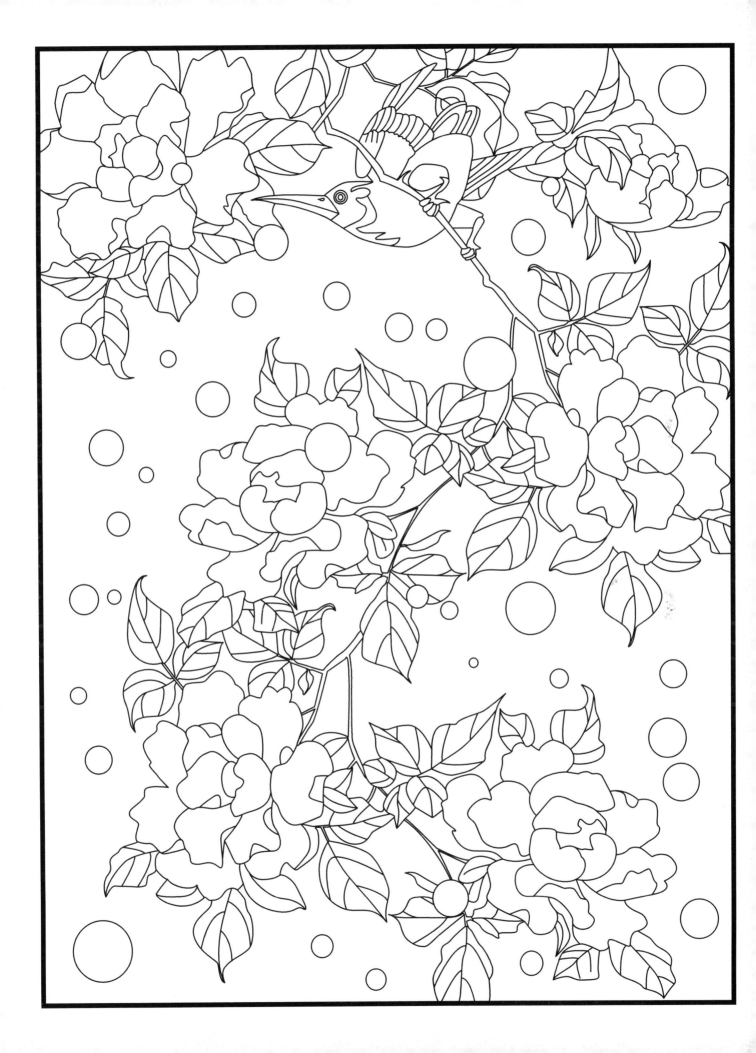

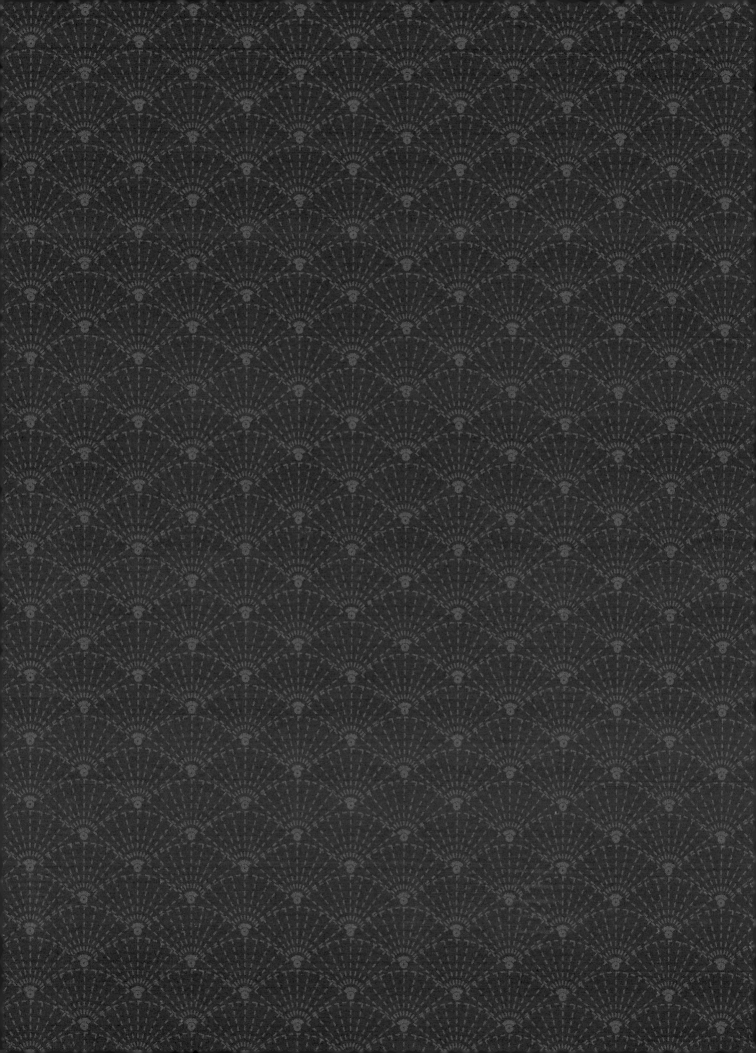

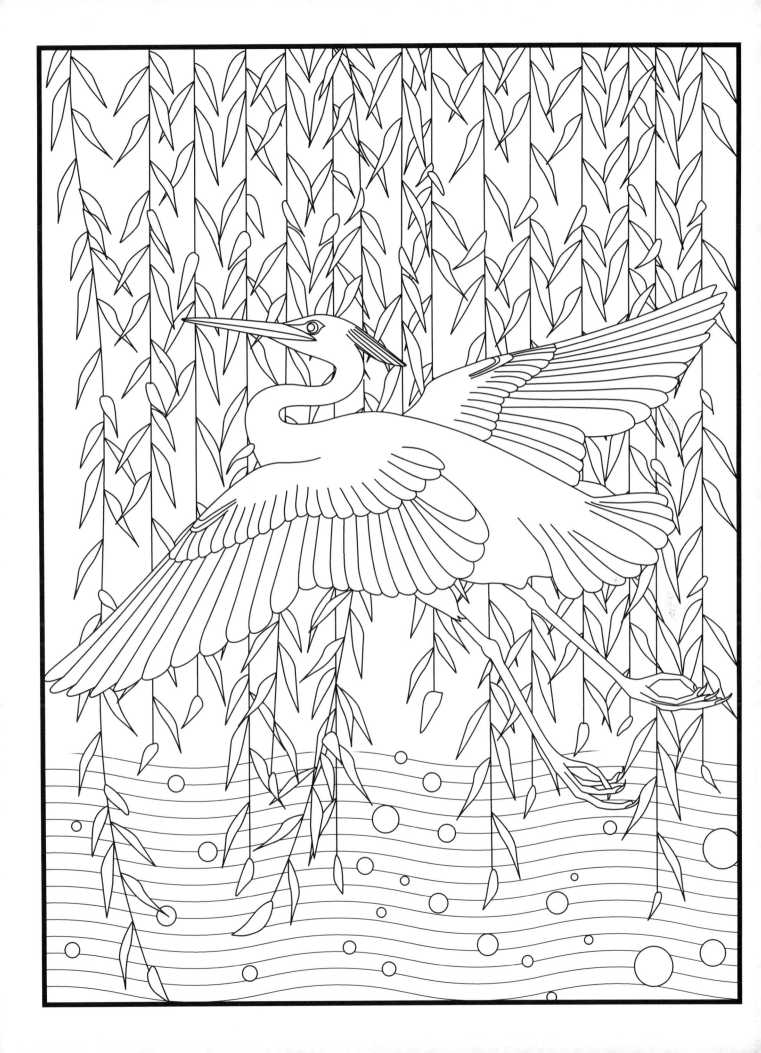

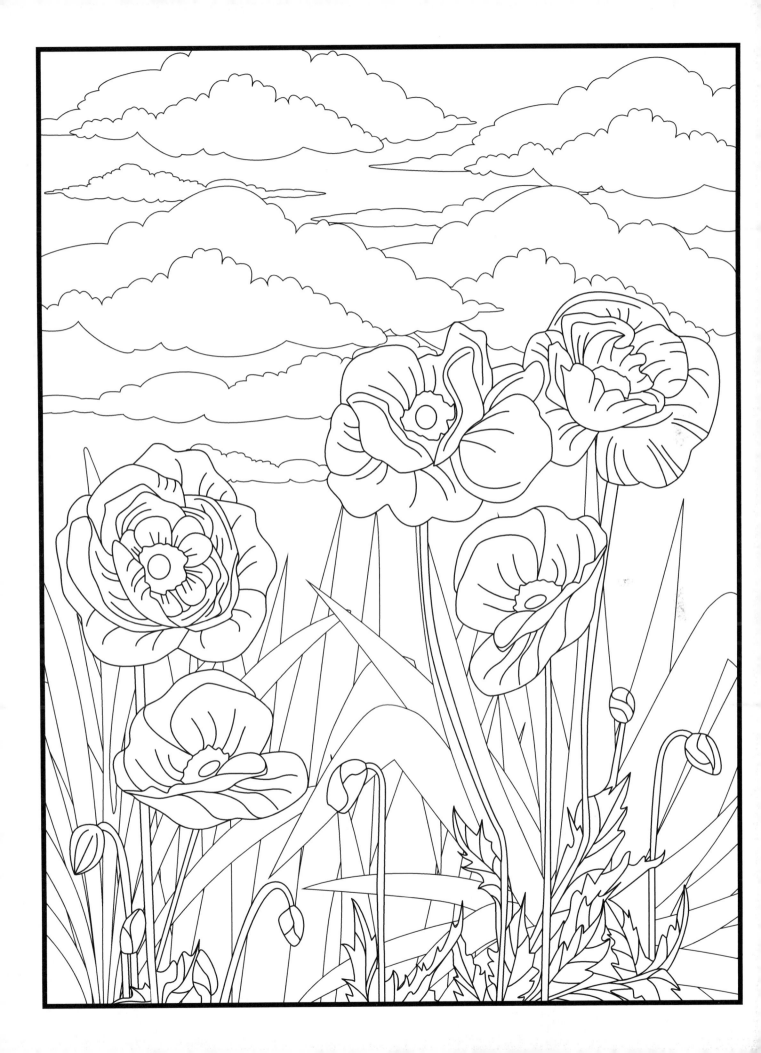

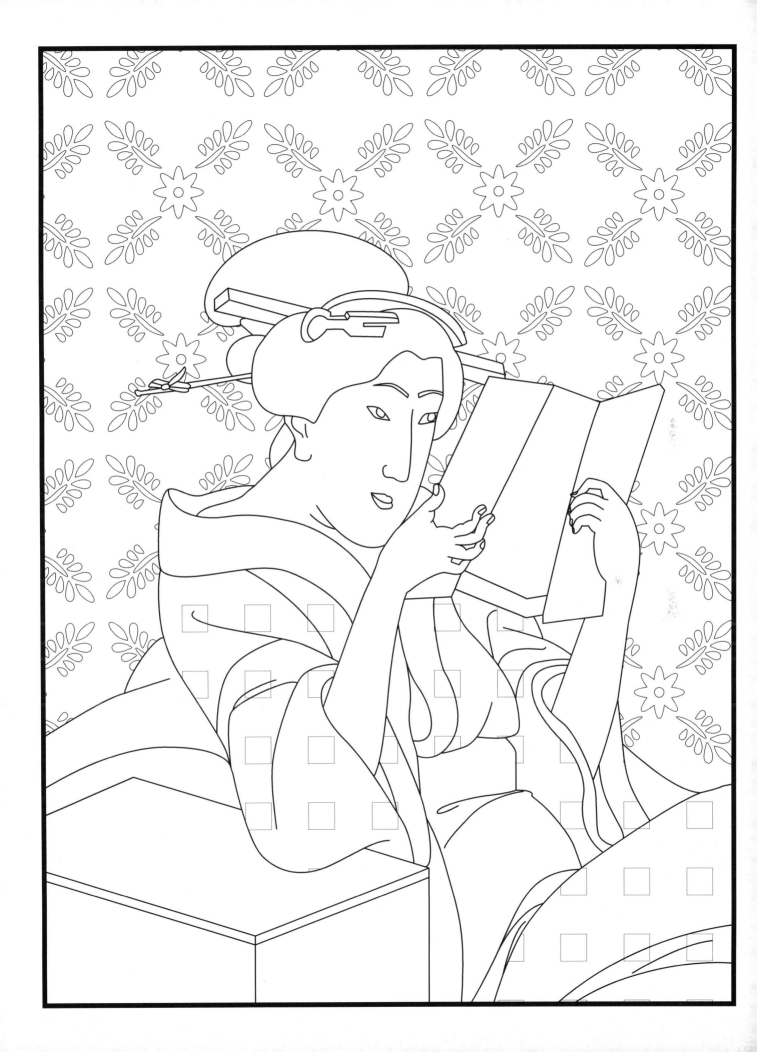

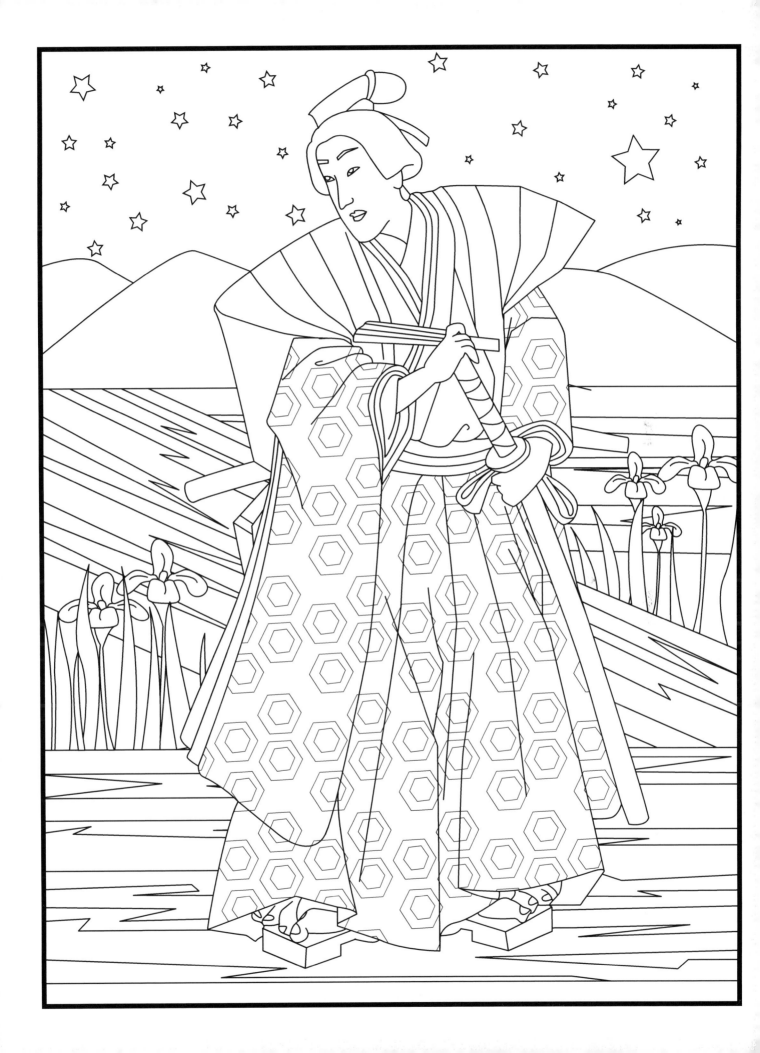

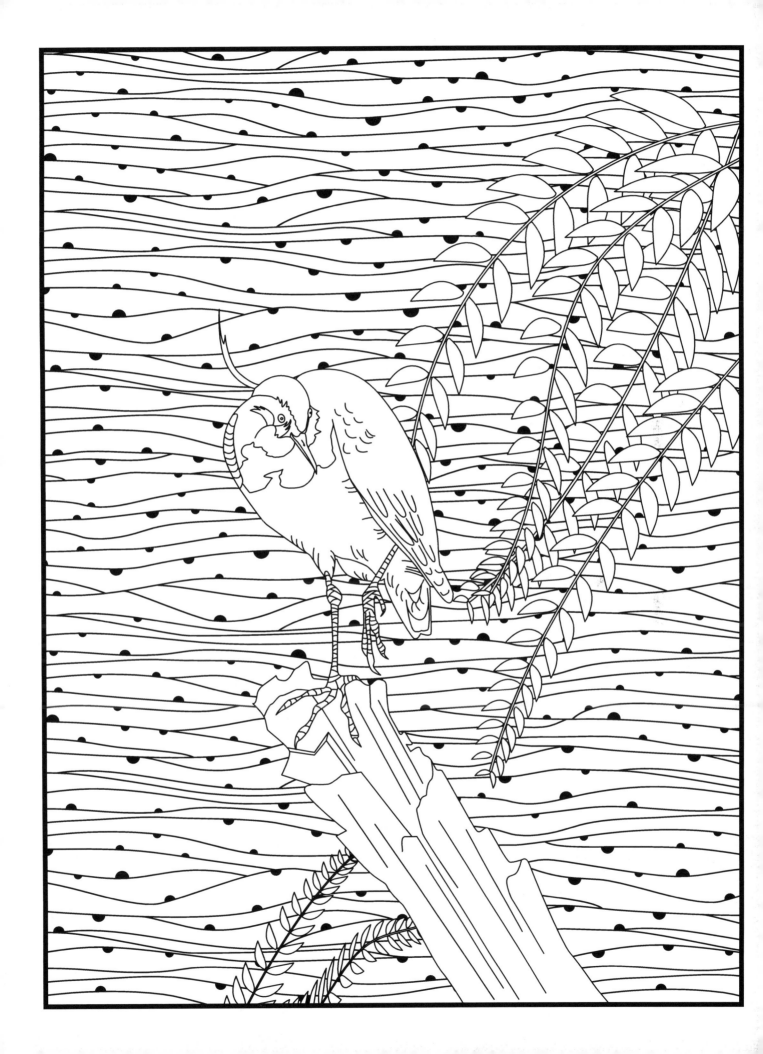

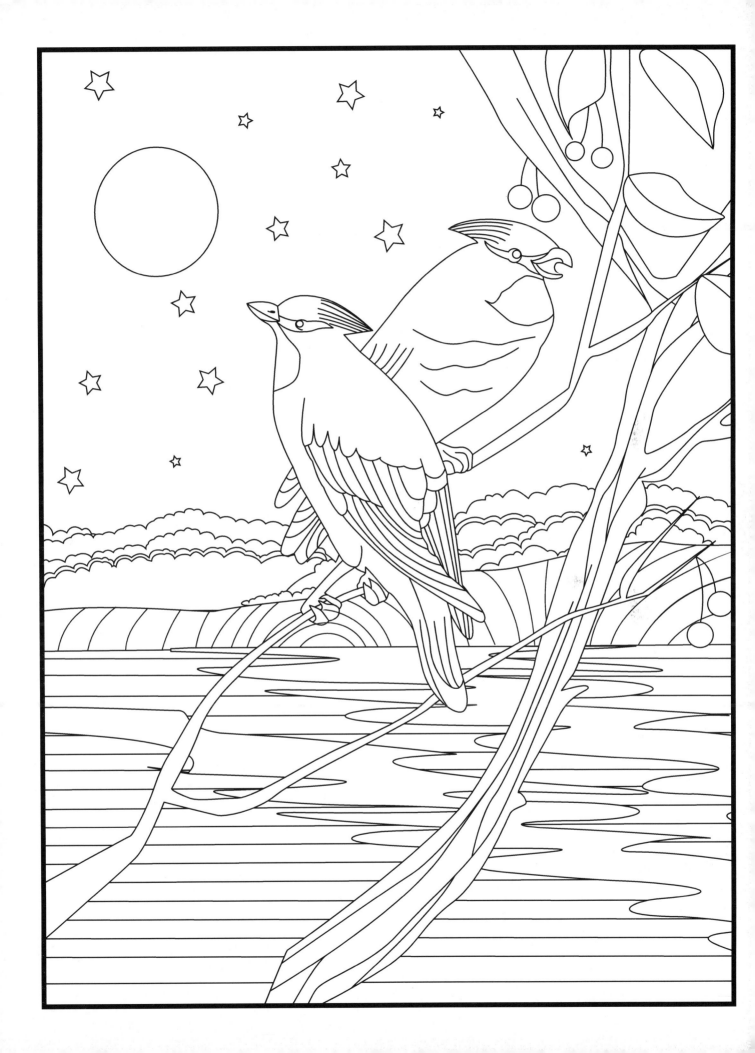

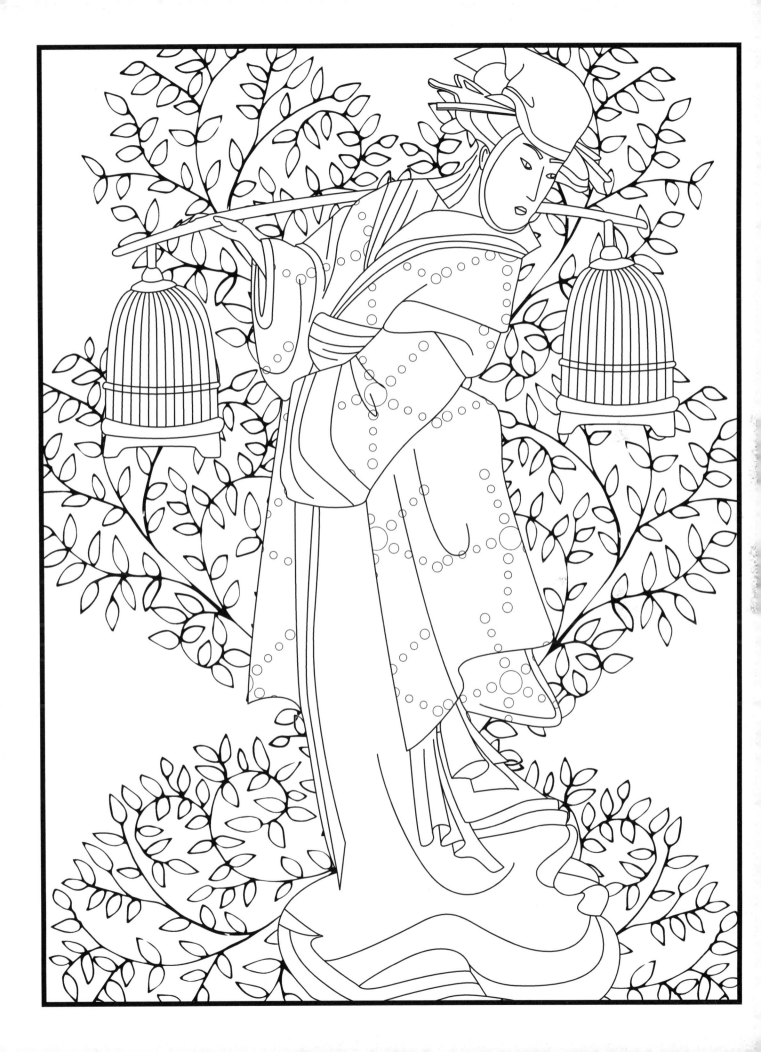

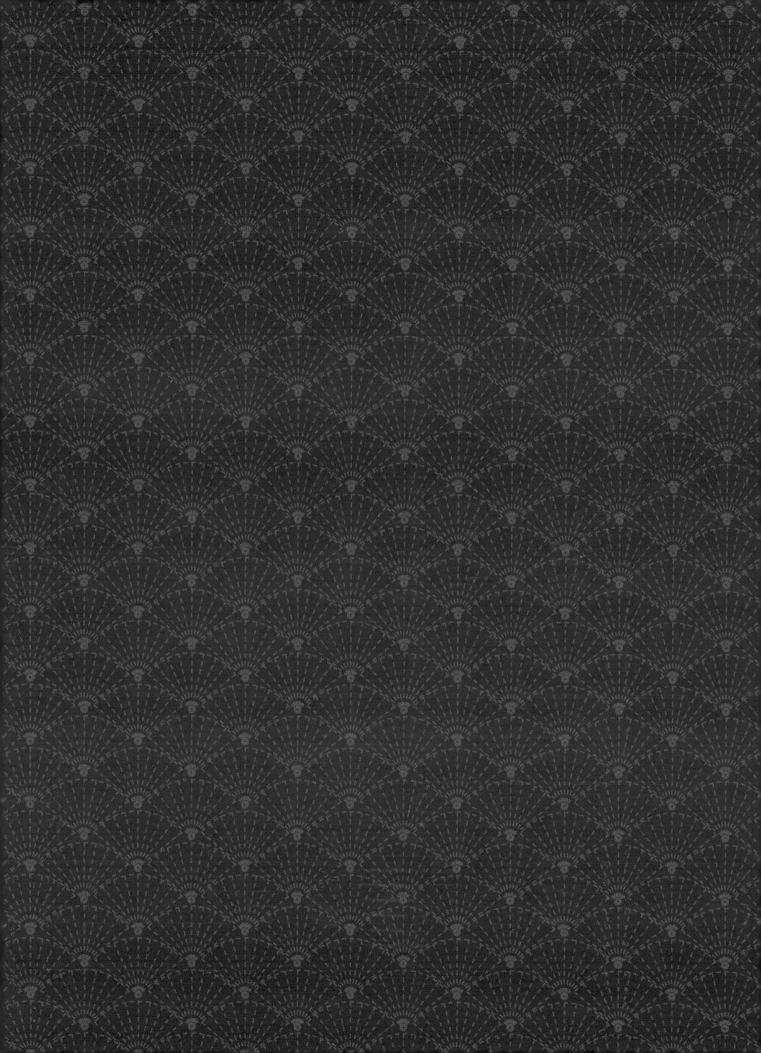

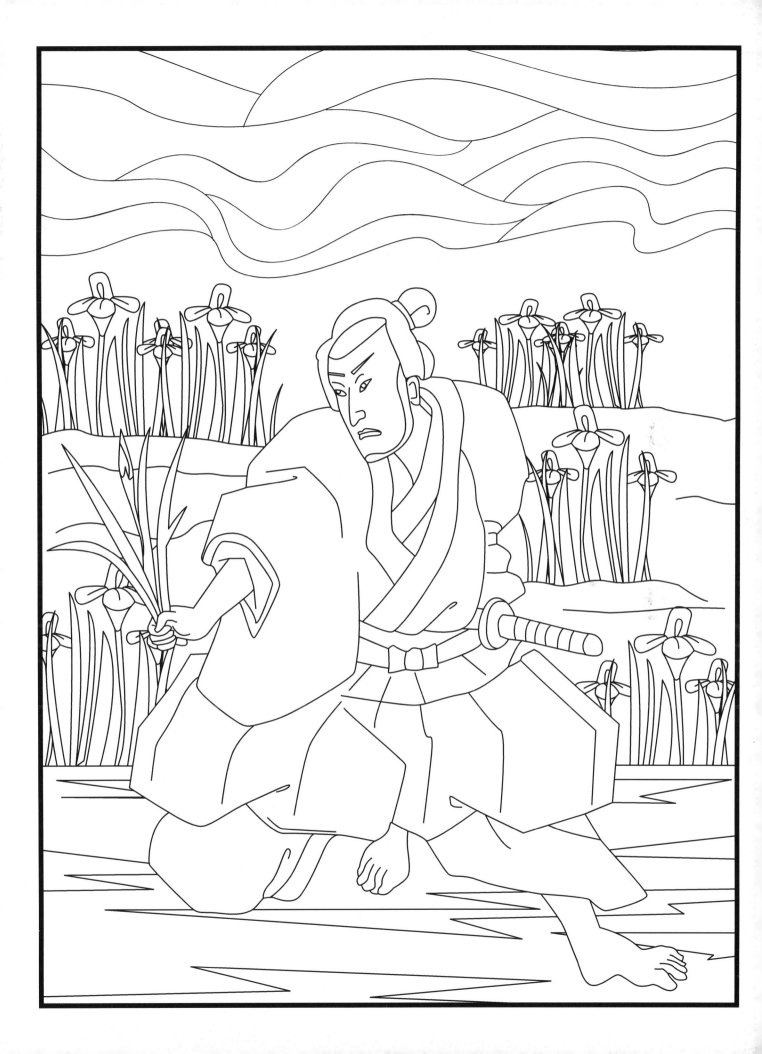

BE SURE TO FOLLOW US ON SOCIAL MEDIA FOR THE LATEST NEWS, SNEAK PEEKS, & GIVEAWAYS

[Instagram] @PapeterieBleu

[Facebook] Papeterie Bleu

[Twitter] @PapeterieBleu

ADD YOURSELF TO OUR MONTHLY NEWSLETTER FOR FREE DIGITAL DOWNLOADS AND DISCOUNT CODES

www.papeteriebleu.com/newsletter

CHECK OUT OUR OTHER BOOKS!

www.papeteriebleu.com

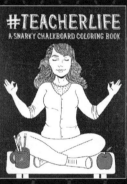 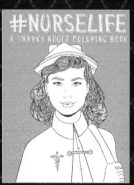 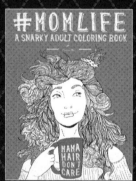 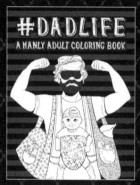 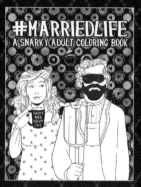

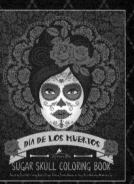 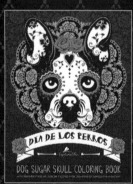 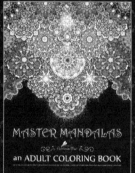 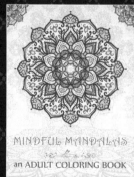 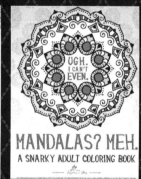

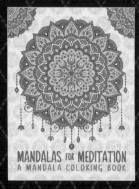 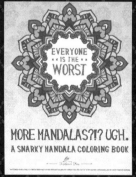 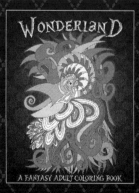

CHECK OUT OUR OTHER BOOKS!

www.papeteriebleu.com

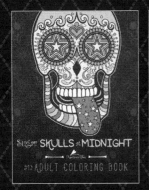

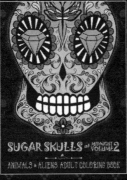

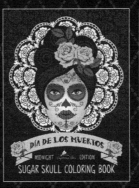

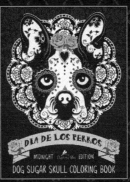

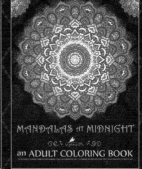

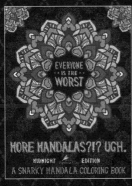

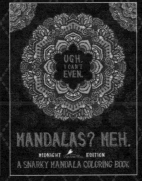

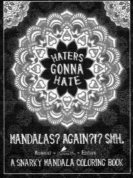

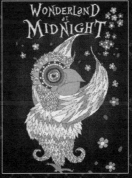

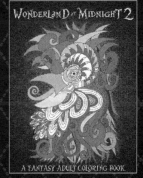

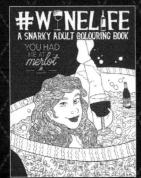

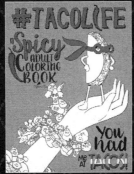

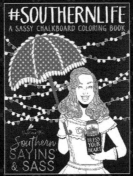

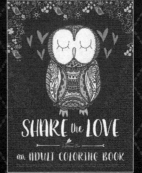

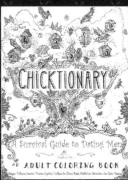

CHECK OUT OUR OTHER BOOKS!

www.papeteriebleu.com

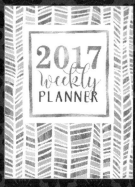 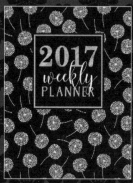 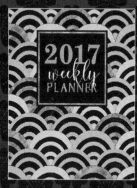 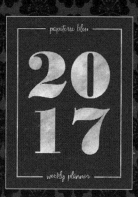 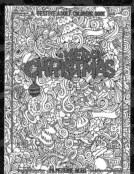

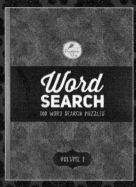 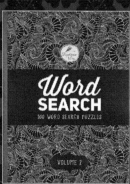 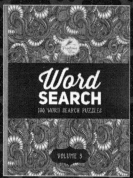 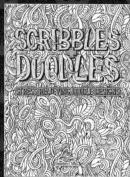 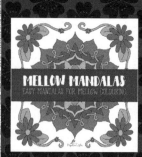

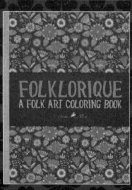 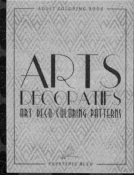 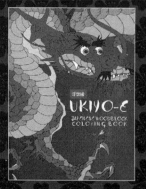